WILD WHEELS

TORINOS

By Michael Portman

Gareth Stevens

Please visit our Web site, www.garethstevens.com. For a free color catalog of all our high-quality books, call toll free 1-800-542-2595 or fax 1-877-542-2596.

Library of Congress Cataloging-in-Publication Data

Portman, Michael, 1976-
 Torinos / Michael Portman.
   p. cm. – (Wild wheels)
 Includes index.
 ISBN 978-1-4339-4756-8 (pbk.)
 ISBN 978-1-4339-4757-5 (6-pack)
 ISBN 978-1-4339-4755-1 (library binding)
 1. Torino automobile. I. Title.
 TL215.T248P67 2011
 629.222'2–dc22

                                   2010039151

First Edition

Published in 2011 by
Gareth Stevens Publishing
111 East 14th Street, Suite 349
New York, NY 10003

Copyright © 2011 Gareth Stevens Publishing

Designer: Christopher Logan
Editor: Therese Shea

Photo credits: Cover, pp. 1, 4-5, 10-11, 12-13, 14-15, 16-17, 18-19, 20-21, 24, 25, 28-29 © Kimball Stock Photo; pp. 2-3 (background), 30-32 (background), back cover (engine), 2-32 (flame border), pp. 6-7 Shutterstock.com; pp. 8-9 Dozier Mobley/Getty Images; pp. 22-23 Kevin Winter/Getty Images; pp. 26-27 iStockphoto.com; pp. 29 (inset) Stan Honda/AFP/Getty Images.

Printed in the United States of America

CPSIA compliance information: Batch #CW11GS: For further information contact Gareth Stevens, New York, New York at 1-800-542-2595.

CONTENTS

Words in the glossary appear in **bold** type the first time they are used in the text.

Think Young

The 1960s were an exciting time for the American automobile industry. Advances in manufacturing made it possible for cars to be smaller, faster, and more comfortable than ever before. The youth market was rapidly growing. Young people wanted cars that were not only powerful and attractive, but also affordable. Carmakers responded with muscle cars.

Muscle cars ruled America's streets during the 1960s and early 1970s.

Muscle cars were fast, fun, and inexpensive. A muscle car is a sporty, midsize car with a powerful engine. Many muscle cars had beginnings as cars **designed** for ordinary daily driving. As demand for high-performance cars grew, automobile companies turned family cars into powerful muscle machines. The Ford Torino was one such car.

INSIDE THE MACHINE

The first true muscle car was the 1964 Pontiac GTO. The GTO was an option package that could be added to Pontiac's midsize car, the Tempest. The GTO was a big success. Soon every other American automobile company was making its own muscle cars.

The Fairlane

In 1955, the Ford Motor Company introduced a full-size car called the Ford Fairlane. The Fairlane was offered in a variety of styles, from a four-door **sedan** to a stylish **coupe**. Like most cars in the 1950s, the Fairlane was big and bulky.

In 1960, Ford completely redesigned the Fairlane. Even though it was bigger and heavier than before, it appeared slimmer and lighter. A year later, another design change gave the Fairlane a sleek and speedy look. It was a sign of the Fairlane's muscle-car future.

Style and comfort were important to fans of the Ford Fairlane.

INSIDE THE MACHINE

The Ford Fairlane was named after Henry Ford's estate in Dearborn, Michigan—Fair Lane. In 1957, the Ford Fairlane became the first mass-produced car series to feature a **hardtop convertible**. The Skyliner, as it was called, was undependable. In 1959, Ford stopped Skyliner production.

The GT

In the 1960s, midsize cars were very popular. In 1962, Ford responded by once again redesigning the Fairlane. This time, it became a midsize car. Despite the smaller size, Ford gave the Fairlane the same high-**horsepower** engines that were used to power full-size cars.

Even though it had a powerful engine, many people didn't consider the Fairlane to be a muscle car. Things began to change in 1966 when Ford introduced the Fairlane GT and GTA. These cars were stylish and fast, but still weren't enough to establish the Fairlane as a true muscle car. Ford wasn't done adding the muscle just yet, though.

INSIDE THE MACHINE

In 1964, Ford produced a special Fairlane—called the Thunderbolt—which was designed for drag races. To lessen the weight of the Thunderbolt, Ford removed almost everything that wasn't necessary for speed, including the side mirrors. Ford produced the Thunderbolt for only a year.

Famous race-car driver Fred Lorenzen drove a Fairlane 427, now found in the International Motorsports Hall of Fame.

The Torino

By the late 1960s, the muscle-car age was in full swing. Ford was enjoying great success with its smaller muscle car—the Mustang—introduced in 1964. Sales of the midsize Fairlane weren't as strong. In 1968, in an effort to improve sales, Ford offered an all-new Fairlane model called the Torino.

The 1968 Fairlanes kept the same 116-inch (295-cm) **wheelbase** from the year before. However, it grew in size everywhere else. When it came to performance, the Torino GT was Ford's midsize champion. Ford offered several engine choices for the Torino GT, including an earthshaking 390-horsepower **big-block engine**!

INSIDE THE MACHINE

The Ford Torino was named after the city of Turin, Italy. Turin—or Torino as it's called in Italian—is the center of Italy's automobile and engineering industries. It's also the home of Italy's largest carmaker, Fiat. Ford briefly considered using the Torino name for its smaller muscle car, the Mustang.

In the name Torino GT, the letters "GT" stand for "Grand Touring." A GT is a comfortable, yet high-performance car.

The Cobra

Ford carried the new high-performance Torino into 1969. Little was changed as far as the car's appearance. However, Ford improved the engines on all Fairlane and Torino models. In 1969, Ford also added a new Torino model fast enough for the track but made for the streets. It was called the Cobra.

While the Torino GT was loaded with features for comfort, the Cobra was just built for speed. Only one engine was available, but it was more than enough. Ford stated that the Cobra's engine—the 428 Cobra Jet—produced 335 horsepower. It actually pumped out closer to 400 horsepower!

INSIDE THE MACHINE

The Cobra name has a long history with Ford Motor Company. In 1961, Ford and Carroll Shelby, a race-car driver and car designer, made the AC Ace British sports car into a powerful race car—the AC Cobra. In addition to this and the Torino Cobra, Ford has used the Cobra name on Mustang models.

The AC Cobra, shown here, was created to beat the Chevrolet Corvette on the racetrack.

The Talladega

During the muscle-car age, there were many ways car companies could get their muscle cars noticed. Eye-catching print ads, movies, and television programs are some examples. One of the best ways, however, was simply to be successful on the racetrack.

In 1969, Ford introduced the Torino Talladega, built for NASCAR (National Association for Stock Car Auto Racing). The Torino Talladega was 5 inches (13 cm) longer than regular Torinos. It was also more **aerodynamic**. This kept the Talladega on the road while it raced at high speeds.

Famous **NASCAR** driver Richard Petty drove Chrysler cars for most of his career. In 1968, however, Petty liked the Ford Torino Talladega so much that he announced a switch. In 1969, he drove a Torino Talladega to 10 victories and finished second in the **NASCAR** championship.

Ford made the Talladega's grille—the grate that allows air in to cool the engine—even with the nose so that air flowed smoothly over the car.

The Torino Talladega faced tough competition on the NASCAR racing circuit in 1969. The Dodge Charger Daytona was the Talladega's biggest rival. However, the Talladega's power and design proved to be superior. The Talladega went on to claim the 1969 NASCAR championship by winning 26 races, including the Daytona 500.

The Torino Talladega's racing success was short lived. Ford only produced the Talladega for a year, although some Talladegas continued to race in 1970. In all, only 745 Torino Talladegas were produced for street use.

The 1969 Torino Talladega is one of the rarest muscle cars.

INSIDE THE MACHINE

In 1969, Dodge created a special aerodynamic car called the Charger Daytona in order to race against Ford in **NASCAR**. In 1970, Ford responded by designing the King Cobra. Unfortunately, only a few King Cobras were ever made, and none ever made it to the racetrack.

Car of the Year

When it was created in 1968, the Ford Torino was just one member of the Ford Fairlane family. In 1970, the Torino became the head of the family. The Fairlane name was given to less expensive Torino models. In addition to rearranging the names, Ford redesigned the Torino for the 1970 model year. The new Torino was longer, lower, and wider than the 1968 and 1969 models.

The Torino GT and Torino Cobra were still part of the family, and the Torino Brougham provided drivers with a touch of **luxury**. *Motor Trend* magazine named the 1970 Ford Torino its Car of the Year.

The 1970 Torino Cobra was heavy for a muscle car, weighing 3,774 pounds (1,713 kg). The added weight may have helped keep the Cobra steady during fast takeoffs. The Torino Cobra could go from 0 to 60 miles (97 km) per hour in just 6 seconds!

The 1970 429 Super Cobra Jet was a sleek muscle car.

Still Strong

For the 1971 model year, Ford made few changes to the Torino's appearance. The muscle-car age was beginning to slow down. Most car companies were reducing engine power. Ford was, too. Although the engine lineup was the same as the year before, Ford lowered the amount of horsepower that most engines produced.

Ford reduced engine power in the 1971 Torinos so that the cars would use less fuel.

The one exception was the Torino Cobra. Ford still gave an option for the powerful 429 Cobra Jet engines that it had given in 1970. However, this was the last year that the Ford Torino fit the label of a true muscle car.

INSIDE THE MACHINE

The 1971 Ford Torino could be ordered in a variety of color combinations, with a selection of 16 colors. In addition to common colors such as white and gold, customers could also choose from colors called Grabber Blue, Grabber Green, and Grabber Yellow.

Changing Times

In 1972, the Ford Torino had its biggest changes yet. It was bigger and heavier than ever before.

The front end was given an oval-shaped grille. It looked like an open fish mouth! In 1972, Ford decided to discontinue the Torino convertible. In 1971, the top engine in a Torino Cobra could pump out 370 horsepower. In 1972, there was no Torino Cobra, and the top Torino engine produced only 248 horsepower.

This 1972 Gran Torino Sport had a place of honor at *The Fast and the Furious* movie opening.

The entire Torino series was renamed for the 1972 model year. A regular Torino was still called a Torino, but the next level Torino was called a Gran Torino. A Torino GT was called a Gran Torino Sport.

INSIDE THE MACHINE

Recently, the Gran Torino has been getting plenty of notice from Hollywood moviemakers. In the **2008** film *Gran Torino*, Clint Eastwood plays a former Ford factory worker who loves his **1972** Ford Gran Torino Sport. A **1972** Gran Torino Sport is also featured in the **2009** film *The Fast and the Furious*.

Time to Go

By 1973, the golden age of the muscle car was over. Rising fuel costs and more safety laws all played a part in its end. Customers were more interested in comfort and **fuel efficiency** than they were in power and speed. Ford steered the Torino and Gran Torino toward the family-car and luxury-car markets.

Car and Driver magazine called a ride in the 1973 Gran Torino Sport "exceptional."

Despite the loss of its muscle-car image, the Ford Torino and Gran Torino continued to sell well from 1972 until 1975. In 1976, Torino sales dropped, and Ford knew it was time to make a change. In 1977, the Torino was replaced by the Ford LTD II.

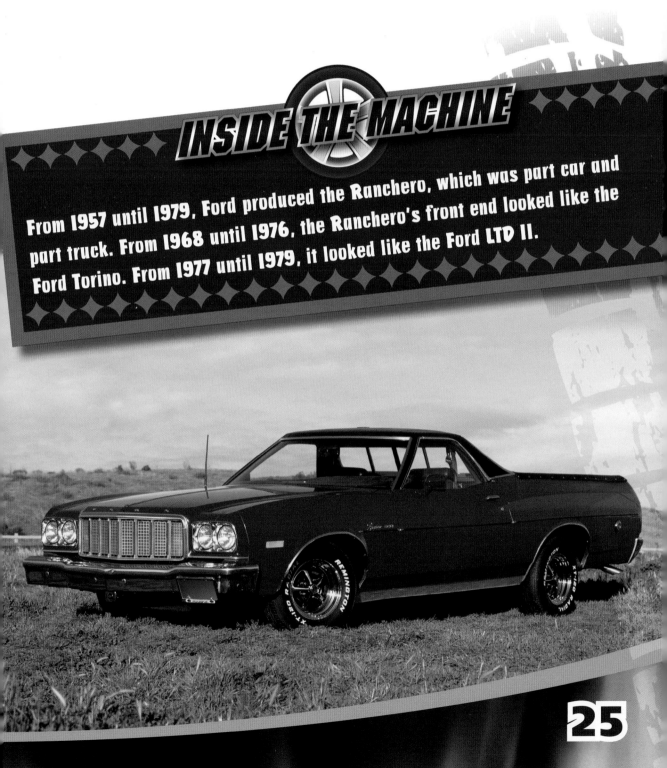

INSIDE THE MACHINE

From 1957 until 1979, Ford produced the Ranchero, which was part car and part truck. From 1968 until 1976, the Ranchero's front end looked like the Ford Torino. From 1977 until 1979, it looked like the Ford LTD II.

Smile for the Camera

In the years before it was discontinued, the Ford Gran Torino had one final spike in popularity. This was thanks to the hit police TV show *Starsky and Hutch*, which began in 1975. The show featured two detectives who cruised the streets of Southern California in a bright red 1975 Gran Torino with a wide, white stripe. In the second season, the two cops upgraded to a 1976 Gran Torino, which they used until the show ended in 1979.

The Gran Torino in *Starsky and Hutch* wasn't really a muscle car, but it looked fast.

The television car was so popular that in 1976 Ford offered a *Starsky and Hutch* Gran Torino. It looked the same as the one used on the show.

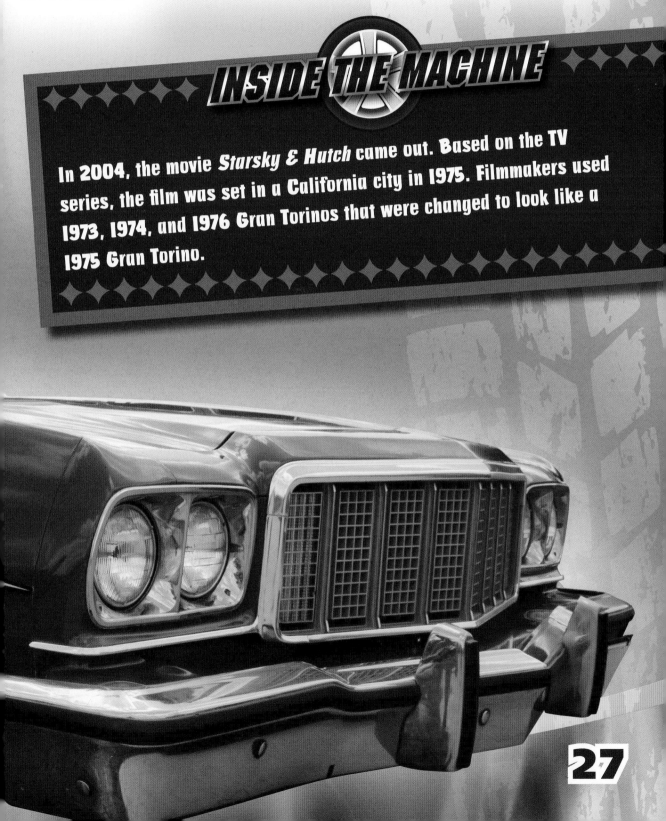

INSIDE THE MACHINE

In 2004, the movie *Starsky & Hutch* came out. Based on the TV series, the film was set in a California city in 1975. Filmmakers used 1973, 1974, and 1976 Gran Torinos that were changed to look like a 1975 Gran Torino.

Still Popular

The Ford Fairlane and Ford Torino were popular cars during the 1950s, 1960s, and 1970s. They offered a wide variety of styles, from convertibles to family cars to street racers, all at an affordable price. However, the Torino Cobra, Torino GT, and Gran Torino were never quite as popular as some of their muscle-car rivals. Despite being larger, the Ford Torino was always overshadowed by the Ford Mustang.

Nevertheless, Ford Torino muscle cars are still popular today. They can be seen at auto shows, in movies, on television, and just driving down the street!

The 1970 Torino Cobra is still loved by muscle-car fans everywhere.

In 2005, Ford unveiled a new Fairlane concept car. Like the original Fairlane, it was big. This Ford had enough seats for seven people. Unlike the original Fairlane, this model was a crossover! This Fairlane, renamed the Ford Flex, went into production in 2008.

Ford Flex

Glossary

aerodynamic: having a shape that improves airflow around a car to increase its speed

big-block engine: a large engine produced in the 1960s and 1970s

concept car: a car built to show a new design and features that may one day be used in cars sold to the public

coupe: a two-door car with one section for the seat and another for storage space

design: to create the pattern or shape of something

drag race: a race between two cars with special bodies and engines on a straight track over a distance of ¼ mile (400 m)

fuel efficiency: the quality of being able to operate using little fuel, or without waste

hardtop convertible: a car that has no center doorpost and has a hard roof that can be lowered

horsepower: a measurement of an engine's power

luxury: the condition of great comfort

option package: extra features that may be bought or may be included in the list of features for a car or truck

sedan: a car with front and back seats, two or four doors, an enclosed body, and a permanent top

wheelbase: the distance between the centers of the front and rear wheels of a car or truck

For More Information

Books

Clarke, R. M. *Ford Torino Performance Portfolio 1968–1974*. Cobham, England: Brooklands Books, 2004.

Woods, Bob. *Hottest Muscle Cars*. Berkeley Heights, NJ: Enslow Publishers, 2008.

Zuehlke, Jeffrey. *Muscle Cars*. Minneapolis, MN: Lerner Publications, 2007.

Web Sites

Collisionkids.org
www.collisionkids.org
Learn about cars by playing games and completing related projects.

Muscle Cars
musclecars.howstuffworks.com
Learn about the mechanics of muscle cars, and see some classic examples.

Muscle Car Coloring Pages 8
www.coloring-pages-book-for-kids-boys.com/muscle-car-coloring-pages.html
See designs and color detailed pictures of some of the most famous muscle cars.

Index